Growing Your Dance Business

by

Anne Walker MBE

Grosvenor House
Publishing Limited

The right of Anne Walker MBE to be identified as the author of this
work has been asserted in accordance with Section 78
of the Copyright, Designs and Patents Act 1988

The book cover picture is copyright to Anne Walker MBE

This book is published by
Grosvenor House Publishing Ltd
Link House
140 The Broadway, Tolworth, Surrey, KT6 7HT.
www.grosvenorhousepublishing.co.uk

A CIP record for this book
is available from the British Library

ISBN 978-1-78623-421-6

Foreword

How often have you heard someone say "oh – it's a dream come true"? Perhaps they've just landed their "dream" job, met their all-time movie hero or won a gold medal at the Olympics. The fact is that we all have dreams. Something in our lives that we want to achieve. Something that turns our hard work and ambition into a gold standard, heart stopping moment of reality. And if you are a dancer, that "dream" could be anything from appearing in a West End Musical, to dancing at Covent Garden, or sharing your skills and passion for dance with others as a teacher.

How brilliant to be able to extend your career by being immersed in the world of dance, as you nurture and inspire a whole new generation of dancers. Watch them grow and mature. See how they revel in the freedom and sheer joy of expression though movement and music, whilst accepting the discipline of technique. And at the same time perhaps discovering your own talent for choreography and production.

It all has the makings of the perfect dream. But of course, could so easily turn into a nightmare without the same sort of preparation, knowledge, discipline and support that you needed to become a dancer in the first place. And no one wants that! Which means that these days in addition to being a dedicated dancer and inspirational teacher – you have to be skilled in the arts of commercial business planning, public relations, social responsibility and a generous helping of unfettered vision and innovation, if in today's economic climate you are going to turn the dream into a commercial success. A good accountant and a friendly bank manager are always great starters for ten. But the knowledge, support, expertise and experience of those who have already been there and done that, with a considerable helping of success, are invaluable. Which is where this book and Anne Walker come in. She's a veritable Dance school Doctor. Her years of experience running her own highly successful dance schools and the internationally successful dancewear company IDS have given her a wealth of insight and experience that is second to none. Her no nonsense approach, over eleven chapters , is chock full of the sort of advice that anyone starting their own dance school, or even wanting to expand the business they already have – will find invaluable.

In common with thousands of professional dancers, or just dance lovers like me, I owe so much to the support, encouragement and skill of my teachers who nurtured me from the age of 4 and introduced me to the sheer joy of being able to dance – be it tap, ballet or jazz. So much so that at the age of 74 I still go to ballet class as part of the silver Swans initiative of the Royal Academy of Dance, for which I am an ambassador. And I see the same delight in a class of mature ladies taking a weekly ballet class as total beginner or experienced "old hands", as I do in my eight year old god-granddaughter concentrating on her work at the barre or cavorting around the studio in free style. In every case, that pleasure and delight comes from the guidance and presence of an inspirational teacher. So as you perhaps consider starting your own business, and becoming a dance school teacher, I wish you luck, I wish you success. But most of all I wish you the personal joy and sheer exhilaration that comes from knowing that you are sharing your passion for and love of dance with a whole new generation that will carry that love into their own futures, and beyond.

Angela Rippon CBE

Acknowledgements

A huge thank you to all my friends and colleagues who have supported me during my many years in the dance industry.

To my wonderful husband and the friends who have encouraged and supported me with this, my first book, thank you from the bottom of my heart.

To you, dear reader, I hope this book proves useful and helps you to follow your dreams as well as growing your business.

I am hugely grateful to Anthony Drewe for his permission to allow me to print his lyrics written for the stage musical of *Mary Poppins*. They have inspired me since I first heard them and I often find myself repeating them.

If you wish to learn more about starting, growing or running your dance business then you can discover more about Anne's Seminars at https://www.annewalker.com

Anne also offers mentoring and coaching via one-to-one meeting or video-call and you can follow her on Facebook at Anne Walker MBE

Contents

Introduction

Running your own dance school is probably something you dreamed about for many years. It is almost certainly something you wanted to do because you had a passion for dance and you wanted to share that with as many people as possible. It is unlikely to have been because you considered it a great way to make loads of money! The chances are, before you set out on the road to owning your own dance school, you did not even consider it as an actual business.

If you do consider yourself a business person, then well done! The vast majority of dance teachers and studio owners do not think of themselves as business people, which is hardly surprising. You must have trained for many hours, indeed years, to learn different genre of dance, new syllabi and techniques, but did you ever spend much time learning any business techniques or how to manage staff, finances or any other aspects of running your own enterprise?

I started my first dance school aged only seventeen, having been inspired by seeing the ballet *Sleeping Beauty* at only eight years old. I certainly went on to learn the hard way. Having had two successful schools, I then founded and, for many years, ran International Dance Supplies which became a multi-million pound global business. It was incredibly hard work, but fun too. I had to re-invent what we did and how we did it on many occasions, but this is what kept everyone focussed.

I want to share with you some of what I learned, so you too, can have a profitable and successful business that gives you the lifestyle you deserve for all the hours and passion you put in to your enterprise.

Dream it, Do it, Make it Happen!

Chapter 1

You Can't Grow Bigger Than Your Dreams

In order to achieve your dreams, you need to know what those dreams actually are. Have you ever sat down and written a list of your goals and aspirations? Do it now!

You can tweak and change your list as time passes, but make the list and keep it safe. It's a good idea to have some simple goals that you can achieve easily, but it's also good to have some big or long-term goals too which can form your vision. You will have a huge sense of achievement when you look back on your list and see what you have achieved.

Your goals may include creating new branches of your school, having your own studio, introducing new genre to the timetable, taking your students to perform overseas, developing your own skills with further qualifications, becoming an examiner or even planning your exit from the business.

Although your list of goals is for your own personal motivation, you will need to share some of those goals in order to make them happen. I started my first dance school when I was only seventeen, I rented various local church halls for a number of years, but I knew I always wanted my own premises. I made sure all my friends and business contacts knew that this was my goal and, by the time I was 21 I had my first business premises with two studios and a changing room plus a small office.

A couple of years later I moved to a better studio in a more central location. Neither of these premises were advertised on the open market, but I was able to acquire them because someone I knew was aware that I was looking for a new home for my dance school. The first studio belonged to the friend of a friend who asked me was I still looking for a studio. It was an old furniture store which had just closed, but was perfect for me at the time.

However, I soon outgrew those premises as my school expanded. Fortunately I had mentioned it to my bank manager. One day he made contact to say another of his clients was looking to rent out two floors of a building and was I interested. Indeed I was!

So share your dreams and aspirations with the local community as well as family, friends and colleagues.

They do not need to know all the details; just enough to keep their eyes and ears open on your behalf. Of course, if you are looking for a studio then you can also contact a commercial property agent, but I doubt if either of my studios would ever have appeared with a letting agent.

Those closest to you should have an idea of your goals as you are bound to require support and encouragement along the way. Your team members also need to have a general understanding otherwise how can they help you achieve those goals? If they understand that you are, for example, aiming for bigger or better premises, then they will realise there is a great future for them in your business. Motivated staff are much more likely to work harder for the good of everyone in the business which will, ultimately, help you achieve your goals as well as helping themselves.

Having aspirations that are generally understood by those around you is good, but others in your local and business community should know too. Everyone knew that my dance school was a professionally run business with ambitions to grow and develop so I was approached by others who offered their support in finding new premises.

It was also important to me to network within the local community. From these contacts I met others who also wanted to work with me and my school and I am sure there were countless recommendations to parents who then sent their children to my ever-growing school. Greater numbers enabled me to run the business more profitably and so I was able to afford my own premises. This would never have happened if I had kept all my goals and dreams to myself.

When I was growing International Dance Supplies (which was called Harlequin Dancewear in the early years) sharing my goals was vital. Even when we were tiny and had only a couple of staff, they knew that the plans were to grow so we could increase our range of products as well as increasing our database of customers. The team knew that brilliant customer service was part of this growth strategy and everyone in the business worked towards delivering the best possible service. They also understood that we had to make a good PROFIT (rather than just a high turnover) in order to achieve our growth and so they then became part of making that happen.

Remember: You can't grow BIGGER than your dreams, so once you get close to achieving your goal, create a new one or even several to cover the next year, five years or even 10 years. If you just have one goal and achieve it, you will find life will just gently bob along! That may suit you, but I believe it is very difficult to "tread water" in business. You either grow with your dreams, or the business fades away.

Even though you may have run your school for many years you need to keep reinventing yourself, as well as the business, in order to stay current and ahead of the competition. Having strong competitors is of great benefit as they will constantly drive you forwards. It is very easy to be complacent if your school is the only one in the area, but if you do have competition, you always need to be one step ahead of them and so your business will continue to evolve and flourish.

The chances are, your ideas will be copied by the other schools but, always remember, imitation is the sincerest form of flattery! Keep your brand strong and your business focussed and you will have nothing to fear. Ensure your team, friends, family and business associates know and understand your goals and then together you can make your dreams come true.

Make It Happen!

1 What is your dream? Write it down now.
2 Write down your one year/two year/five year goals.
3 Believe you can make them happen.
4 Start to share these goals with people around you.
5 Remember: You can't grow bigger than your dreams, so dream as big as you dare!

Chapter 2

This is a Business

Do you think of yourself as a business person, or a dance teacher? Do you consider yourself a professional, or a dance teacher?

You are most definitely all of these, but not many dance teachers talk about "my business" or "my profession". They are much more likely to say, "I am going to dancing," or "I am going to teach". Do you do this? It is vitally important that all dance teachers realise they are professionals and are running a business. Without that mind-set, it is unlikely that other businesses, parents or the general public will treat dance teachers as business owners. Omitting to talk about what you do as a business is not at all helpful to your school, or to the industry in general.

You have trained for many years to become a dance teacher and you continue to learn new syllabi or genres. You pay insurance, rent and taxes like everyone else and you have to contend with many other costs because you work with young people as well as recorded music.

You are definitely running a business, so you must ensure that is obvious to everyone.

Think about some great businesses which you love and admire. What aspects of those businesses appeal to you? Do you like their customer service or the way they make you feel like a valued customer? Do you always get a warm welcome and a "smiley" voice, even if you are dealing with that business via phone? Do they sound and look professional? Can you use some of those attributes in your own business?

WEBSITE

Ensure your business website reflects your vision and your brand.

- Is your website address the same as your school name?

- If your website is old it may be worth having a refresh, making sure that it works well on mobile phones and tablets. You will probably find that the majority of people who access your website do so via mobile or tablet so be sure your website works well on a small screen as well as on a laptop or PC.

- If you are considering having a completely new website then it is vital that you are able to make simple updates to it yourself. It can be a very basic but informative site, but there is nothing that shouts, "this is not a serious business," more than an out of date website.

- Maybe you post updates on social media, rather than on your website, but a prospective parent looking at your out of date website will turn to your competitor in an instant.

- Having a new website could also give you the opportunity to rebrand or at least have a relaunch party or event which could generate some great publicity as well as make everyone realise your business is flourishing and keeping abreast of the times.

- A rebrand or relaunch is just the sort of story the local press and media would love, so write a press release and send it, with photographs, to as many papers, magazines and radio stations as possible, as well as talking about your relaunch on social media and via customer emails.

DOMAIN NAME

- Your domain name must be owned by you rather than a kind parent who set up your original website a few years ago! Make sure you know where your domain is hosted and by whom.

Hopefully you already do own your domain name so you will be able to use email addresses linked to this domain. If you need further information you should be able to look it up here (for UK names) https://www.nominet.uk/whois . If you want to find global addresses or to purchase a domain then one of the companies to check with is https://uk.godaddy.com.

- It may also be worth checking to see if the .com or even .uk addresses are available too. You may think they are not relevant but it could well save you from an unscrupulous competitor trying to divert some of your web enquiries from your website to theirs. You would be amazed at the lengths some people will go to in order to get more business; especially if they can steal some of what should be *your* business.

I have seen this happen on a number of occasions and it will be much more expensive to buy the domain name back from an unscrupulous person than ever it would have been to buy it yourself in the first place.

EMAIL ADDRESS

- As you have a professional and business-like email address, please **use it** and do not use a silly one like anne1978@gmail.co.uk. Why on earth would you advertise Google every time you write your email address when you could be promoting your own business? For FREE!

- If your school web address is www.annewalker schoolofdance.co.uk you will be able to use anne@annewalkerschoolofdance.co.uk as your email address. You may also like to use enquiries@ or office@ so you can track where your emails originate.

SOCIAL MEDIA

- Social media is pretty important these days but remember that this is part of your business communication so ensure you (or whoever is responsible for writing posts) are using correct spelling, grammar and punctuation. It reflects badly on the professionalism of your brand if there are typos or errors with a stray apostrophe.

- It is a completely wasted business opportunity if you fail to use any form of social media. You may not want more students or you may not think you have time to post updates on social media, but always remember that your competitors WILL find the time and gradually, over time, it will be your brand that diminishes. All businesses need to have their name kept in the public eye.

Subliminally, people are aware of what your school is achieving and how it fits in to your community and the dance world.

- Take the time and trouble to plan your use of social media and it can pay dividends in brand awareness which will result in new students – or a waiting list if you already have enough students! And remember: you can schedule your posts, if you take the time to set up a handful of posts, you can schedule them to be posted over the course of the next few days or even weeks. 30 minutes of your time now will give you FREE publicity for days or weeks to come. Try it!

EMPLOYING PEOPLE

- Because this is a business, you must ensure you comply with employment law.

- Deciding if the members of your team are employed or self-employed can be tricky, but for businesses in the UK, there is an extremely useful government website which offers huge amounts of clarification and help. The home page is here: https://www.gov.uk and information relating to employed versus self-employed can be found here: https://www.gov.uk/employment-status/selfemployed-contractor

- It is definitely worth checking to make sure you should not be employing someone, rather than paying them as though they were self-employed. As the business owner this is your responsibility and you could end up having to pay if you get it wrong.

POLICIES AND PROCEDURES

There is more detail in Chapter eight but here are some basics you must consider.

- Policies and procedures are essential to any well run business. In this world of working with children we have even more policies to consider but, once you have them all in place, then all it takes is an annual "tweak" to ensure you are in line with the law and as business-like as possible.

- Some of the policies you should consider (in some countries these may be mandatory):

  Health & Safety Policy (including risk-assessment)
  Child Protection/Safeguarding Policy
  Equal Opportunities Policy
  GDPR/Data Protection Policy
  Cookie Policy
  Customer Service Policy
  Grievance Policy

You will also need to consider licences for playing music both in class and at performances.

Templates and examples of policies for use in UK may be found here:

http://www.hse.gov.uk/simple-health-safety/write.htm

https://learning.nspcc.org.uk/safeguarding-child-protection/writing-a-safeguarding-policy/

https://www.gov.uk/browse/employing-people

http://www.acas.org.uk

https://cdmt.org.uk/part-time-learning/apply-now

https://pplprs.co.uk

For readers in Scotland:

https://www.bgateway.com/business-guides has loads of useful advice and most countries will offer this sort of support from their government website.

NETWORKING

- Aim to network with other business people and not just people in the dance industry.

- Join a local business-networking group and talk to other business owners. You will soon realise they have many of the same challenges that you have even though you may operate in a very different sector. By sharing stories and solutions you could well gain some new ideas to solve some of your business problems.

- If you are looking for a new accountant, bank or lawyer a networking event is often a great place to meet new supplier businesses. You can then talk to the people from these businesses and see with whom you could build a business relationship. Possibly other business owners would be able to make recommendations to you too.

- Make sure you ALWAYS have business cards with you. You never know when you might meet someone who could be helpful to your business or who may be looking for a dance teacher. If you can give them your business card with your website and contact details it immediately makes you look business-like and professional.

Make It Happen!

1 Remember this is a BUSINESS.
2 Check your website is in the name of your business.
3 Check your email is in the name of your business.
4 Set a date to review your Policies & Procedures every year.
5 Never leave home without your business cards.

Chapter 3

Your Business. Your Vision

We have established you are running a business, and you know and understand what your goals are. You need to keep focussed on this – constantly! Starting, running or growing a business is never an easy option! It takes years of hard work and determination and you absolutely must be focussed on your goals in order to make them happen.

As well as your short- and long-term goals you need a VISION for your business that is going to be the reason you continue to do what you do. It will be your reason for getting up each morning and the reason you carry on when life seems to be especially challenging.

Create a Vision Statement for your business. This should be your hopes and dreams at the highest level. It should be aspirational, but also something that everyone in the business can believe in and feel they can be connected with, in some way. Weave your purpose, goals and values in to your vision statement, keep it short and make it unique to you.

Under Steve Jobs, Apple's vision statement was, "To make a contribution to the world by making tools for the mind that advance humankind". Nike Inc.'s is, "to bring inspiration and innovation to every athlete in the world." My vision statement at IDS (International Dance Supplies) was for us to have, "Global domination of the Dancewear Industry" and of course, Walt Disney's was, "To make people happy".

What will yours be?

You know what your vision is for your business, so do not allow others to distract you or persuade you to do things differently. This is *your* business. A parent in your school discussing the needs of their child with you is only focussed on that child. You must have the same single-minded outlook, but with your focus on your business.

A suggestion from a parent may sound like a good idea, but you must be very sure it is the best thing for your business before you even consider changing something. It can be a huge challenge not to do as requested when faced with a group of people who want you to do something differently. If it works for the business, fine, otherwise hold your nerve!

Pressure may also come from members of your team. You should certainly listen to their ideas, but then you must make a decision based on the needs of your business and your vision. This is one of the fundamental reasons for having your team completely engaged with your vision. If they know what, and how, you are planning to achieve, they are much more likely to make useful and positive suggestions rather than just thinking about what would benefit them personally. Worse still, they may not consider the long-term effects of their suggestion and how it could impact on turnover or profit.

The more business-like your school appears, the less likely you are to have to explain your decisions or policies to other people. If everyone in your local community, as well as parents, students and staff, see that you are running a well-organised business, they will never question your decisions. Whereas, if your school looks like your hobby rather than your main income, people are much less likely to treat what you do with the seriousness you expect or require.

If you often find yourself defending your decisions to parents and colleagues, perhaps it is time to take a serious look at the way you present your business to the big wide world:

- Does it really reflect your vision, your passion and your brand?
- Does it look like a professional business to your local community and other business owners?
- Do your accountant, lawyer and bank recognise you as a professional business-owner?

If you feel there is room for improvement, then you must change some of your ways of working. It will not improve without some changes.

This may be a challenge for you, but if it results in greater awareness of your school as a serious enterprise, it will have been worth the effort. Once you have decided to make changes then stick to your decision and *do not apologise* for it! This is *your* business.

You should always "sell" a change as a benefit. Most people are scared of change of any sort but there is always a positive. You should point out how this change will make their life (or that of the student) better/easier/simpler, or even enable them to achieve more. Deliver this information to everyone in a positive and upbeat manner. If you are imparting this information via email, ensure the subject line is positive (and short).

If you are saying it, then make sure you have a bright tone of voice rather than an apologetic one and SMILE. If this information is going out in a letter to parents ensure you list the BENEFITS of the changes and *do not apologise.*

It is essential that you continue to evolve your business. A business that does not change with the times will ultimately fail. Just as you should "tweak" your goals and dreams, so you may want to "tweak" the vision for your business.

Maybe look at a sector that you have never before considered teaching: Adult Ballet, Mums and toddlers, wheelchair users, deaf students. Or you could consider teaching dance to those with Alzheimer's or Parkinson's. This could give your school a whole new lease of life and will very likely have a positive impact on many others at your school as well as within your local community. As well as training to teach any of the above you could of course learn to teach something completely different such as acro or gymnastics. This may be a great opportunity for one of your teachers to retrain too.

This is *your* business and you must run it in a way that supports the best interests of you and the whole business. Once you start to practice some of these positive steps you will reap the rewards.

Make It Happen!

1 Create a **Vision Statement** for your business.
2 Remain focussed on your goals and your vision for the future.
3 Encourage your team to think about how they impact on your business and its vision.
4 Do not apologise for your vision.
5 Believe in your vision and yourself.

Chapter 4

Your Brand

What springs to mind when you think of a brand? Do you think of a logo? A name? A tag-line? A colour? Branding is about all those but also so much more!

The Business Dictionary definition of branding is:

"The process involved in creating a unique name and image for a product in the consumers' mind, Branding aims to establish a significant and differentiated presence in the market that attracts and retains loyal customers".

Isn't that exactly what you want! You want your customers, and potential customers, to understand why your school is unique and why students should come to your school for the best possible experience. Once they are part of your school, you need to keep them there. So, the stronger your brand, the better your chances are of building and growing your business.

What is your brand?

- Do you know what your USP (unique selling proposition) is?
- What is your tag-line (if you have one)?
- What does your brand "look" like?
- Can you describe its "texture"?
- What does it "smell" like?
- What colour is it?

Can you answer all these questions quickly and easily? If you asked your students the same questions what would they say? How would the parents respond? How would the rest of your team (teachers, assistants, receptionist) respond?

If there are many very different answers to these questions it will be very challenging to ensure your brand is as strong as it can be in order to grow and retain your student numbers. Sometimes even the basics are not known by parents or students. If they only ever see "Miss Julie" teaching, they may not actually realise that the school is called "Walker School of Dance" unless your branding is obvious. If you can strengthen your brand awareness you will discover that it:

- Builds brand loyalty from your students and parents.

- Makes it easier for people to interact with you.
- Is subliminal advertising at every touch point.
- Means students are more likely to remain in your school for longer.

Everyone wants to belong to a club, group or "family" and, by having a strong brand, your students will really feel part of your school.

If you have a strong name and logo that is quickly and easily recognised by everyone inside and outside the business, then well done! Have you changed it all in the last five years or has it looked pretty much the same for the last 20 years? Even though the name will probably not change, it is always a good idea to "tweak" the logo from time to time, just to keep it fresh and current.

Do you have a tag line? It is not always necessary but can be useful to define or clarify what your business actually does, if that is not obvious from the name. For example, if you are called "XX School of Dance", it is pretty obvious what the business is all about. However, if you are called "XX Academy" you could be confused with an educational school so it might be useful to have a tag line which explains what genres or ages you teach. A tag line can be easily altered as the school grows or develops without having to have an expensive name change. If you do have one, remember to use your tag line on your website, social media and wherever it is appropriate. It should be an integral part of your brand.

How can you reinforce your brand and develop it to run through everything you do? There are many simple solutions:

- Make sure your website is in the name of your school in order to reinforce your brand.

- Use an email address that is based on your website. For example; if you own www.walker schoolofdance.com then your email address should be anne@walkerschoolofdance.com and NOT anne1976@bt.com

- Have a school uniform that is unique to you. Leotards as well as hoodies, etc. can be printed with your school name or logo to reinforce your brand. Other branded items will make your students as well as teachers feel they really are part of your team and "family". Even your adult classes will feel more engaged with your brand if they have some sort of "uniform" T-shirt or top.

- As well as using your logo on absolutely all printed material, documents, business cards, flyers, signage, and website, try and stick to one or two main typefaces and one or two main colours in order to reinforce your brand.

- Is there scope to display a banner or poster outside your studio? Even if you use different halls on different days of the week, it should be possible to have some sort of poster or advertisement which should reflect your brand.

- If you teach in rented halls it should still be possible to have some sort of noticeboard or at least a sign with the name of your school, as well as some of the important information to which everyone should have access.

- How is your phone answered? This is part of your branding too! If you or a family member sometimes answers your phone with just a "hello" or a gruff voice, that is not doing anything at all for your brand or your professionalism.

- Your telephone voicemail should have a simple message with your school name and any other details clearly spoken.

- If you are not available to answer emails quickly, then make sure you have an "out of office" message which tells people how quickly they can expect a response.

All these details add to your professionalism and the seriousness of your business as well as growing your brand awareness in your community.

Creating a strong brand for your business will ensure it stands out from your competitors as well as building a strong and loyal band of supporters. Be proud of what you and your business stand for, and your team will be proud of it too.

Make It Happen!

1 Remember what your brand is, and what it stands for.
2 Keep focussed on your USP.
3 Ensure your branding is obvious on all websites, emails, signage, documents, etc.
4 Reinforce your branding on uniform for students and teachers.
5 Be proud of your brand and USP.

Chapter 5

Your Team

If you are lucky enough to have some support from other teachers or assistants in your school then you must make sure you look after them!

Your team may consist of employed teachers, freelance teachers, class assistants, office staff or consultants and you need to know how to treat them all and what sort of support and training they will require. Your team may also include your own parents, partner or children who may field phone calls at home. Remember to include them in training too!

Firstly you must ensure that it is legal for any proposed member of staff to be working in your country and your profession. In the UK, at the time of writing, the government requires you (the employer) to ensure that they have a right to work in the UK and for those working with young people a DBS (Disclosure and Baring Service) check. Information and support is available here: https://www.gov.uk/employing-staff

If your business is in Scotland information is available here: https://www.bgateway.com/business-guides

Other countries also provide their own requirements via a government portal or website. As the employer, or potential employer, it is your responsibility to make these checks. Ignorance is NOT bliss and would be inadmissible as an excuse if ever your actions were queried by an inspector or law enforcement agency.

It is also vitally important that you are certain any staff who plan to be self-employed, are legally entitled to hold that status, if they are, they then become liable for any tax or national insurance due. However, if there is any doubt whatsoever in your mind, you should seek professional advice from an employment lawyer.

Another consideration before taking on any staff is to ask yourself the question, "can I afford to pay someone?" Apart from their fee or salary you will need to ensure their safety and wellbeing, guard against discrimination and keep their data safe in line with GDPR (General Data Protection Regulation).

Once you have agreed on your staff and their status you need to have a written contract with them as well as a job description. For schools in the UK, the Council for Dance, Drama and Musical Theatre www.cdmt.org.uk

has examples of both an employed and self-employed contract which you can download and personalise with your own branding. They also have a number of other useful policies which you can use within your business without having to pay legal fees to have one drawn up. Please make sure you personalise them with your own branding. Their Code of Professional Conduct for Teachers may also be useful. Once the contracts have been signed and returned to you, ensure you keep them in a safe and secure manner and remember to refer to them if ever a dispute arises.

In order to ensure your team know and understand your brand and your goals, you should have various training, coaching or inspirational sessions for them. If they are employees then six-monthly appraisals and reviews are essential too. If you have a mixture of employed and self-employed it is a good idea to have some sort of gathering, either each term or biannually, where they can all meet and mix. This is especially important if your school is spread over a wide geographical area and the teachers do not meet regularly when teaching. Possibly you and they teach at the same time so you do not often have the opportunity to discuss school business.

If you have a "training day" or a "team day", you could perhaps provide a few hours of mentoring, then some new work providing them with useful CPD (Continuing

Professional Development), followed by a fun afternoon tea, supper or a night out that could bring your team together and help them all to move forward along your brand and business guidelines.

It is also important that your team know they can raise new ideas or problems with you and that you will give them a fair hearing. If they are employed then they will need their own goals and objectives but make sure these are **SMART** (Specific, Measurable, Achievable, Realistic and Time-bound). Do not just tell the teacher you want the Grade 2s to take an exam. In order to make it **SMART** you should tell them you want the Grade 2 class to:

- **Take their Grade 2 exam** (Specific)
- They either will, or will not take exam (Measurable)
- They are being correctly taught (Achievable)
- They attend a Grade 2 class (Realistic)
- **By the end of March next year** (Timebound)

Just like your students, the team need to know what their boundaries are and how you will help them to work within those boundaries. They, and you, should adhere to a professional code of conduct which is generally provided by the dance awarding body with whom you gained your qualifications. If you want to have your own for the school then CDMT (Council for Dance, Drama and Musical Theatre) has one on their website you can use: https://cdmt.org.uk/part-time-learning/apply-now. As with all policies, you should review it on an annual basis and make any appropriate changes.

If any team member talks to you about any problems or challenges they may be having, be certain to make a time to sit down and discuss these issues with them. If you ignore them, hoping they will go away, any small problems are likely to get larger. It is important that you allow them to discuss this with you and equally important you are seen to respect their views. You can then make an informed decision about the next steps. Your business will be stronger if you listen.

It is also crucial that you encourage all of your team to undertake CPD (Continuing Professional Development). They must realise the importance of continuing to develop their own skills and how it has an impact on developing the skills of the students they teach. Techniques move on and teaching methods change with time. You and they must make changes accordingly in order to help your school grow and flourish.

Health and safety is a key area of your responsibility as a business owner. You must ensure everyone who works with and for you, has a good knowledge of your Health and Safety Policy. They should also fully understand all procedures, including essentials such as how to report an accident, evacuation procedures, etc. Although your team have a duty of care to maintain safe working practices it is your responsibility to ensure your Health and Safety Policy is current and adhered to, at all times, by everyone.

Your team should understand risk assessments and how they relate to your business. On occasions they may be the one to be filling in a risk assessment form so you must make sure they understand this and know their responsibilities. They are responsible for any children they are teaching during lesson time, it is vital all your team understand their obligations to the students as well as to you, the business owner.

Sometimes an employee or freelance teacher is just not the right fit for your business. If this is the case, do not continue to have them on your team just because it's the easy option. This will probably be damaging your business and your brand much more than you realise. Face the facts and deal with the situation as soon as possible.

Generally that person will realise all is not well and they will probably be very unhappy. Undoubtedly they will be making the pupils they teach and, potentially, colleagues unhappy too. Talk to them as soon as you realise there is a problem. Give them a chance to explain if there are any problems and you may be able to reach a solution.

If you cannot improve the situation you may have to ask them to leave. It is only hard the first time you do this and afterwards the atmosphere will probably be much more positive. If it is the right thing for your business you must make it happen!

Details of all employment laws will vary in different countries so appropriate professional advice should always be taken from an employment lawyer. In some places local business groups may offer free, or subsidised, advice or support on these and other business matters. In the UK the FSB (The Federation of Small Businesses) https://www.fsb.org.uk/ has some great support which can save you more than the cost of the membership fee if you use their services. The government website https://www.gov.uk also has masses of really helpful advice for anyone who is governed by UK law.

Make It Happen!

1   Check that all your team have signed and returned their contracts to you.
2   Organise team gatherings either each term or biannually.
3   Have brand awareness sessions with your team.
4   Encourage your team to share their challenges with you.
5   Deal with any issues as soon as they arise – problems get larger the longer they are avoided!

Chapter 6

Marketing and Communication

Even though you probably obtain many of your new students by word of mouth, marketing still plays a huge role in growing your business and good communication both inside and outside your business will help you continue to grow and expand.

Marketing and Communication are both key to your business, but they must both be completely enmeshed in, and with, your brand.

Many things about marketing and communication are common sense but in the general panic of day-to-day life the obvious can sometimes be overlooked. You should remember that every time you write something somewhere you are COMMUNICATING, so whether you are writing on your website, social media, an email, or a letter to parents, you must always remember certain basic rules.

1 **WIFM**. This is one of the most important things to remember as everyone is really only interested in **What's In It For Me**! No matter how much, or how well, you write, if it is not immediately obvious how what you are saying is of BENEFIT to the reader, you will quickly lose their interest. Think about this next time you send out a message relating to fees/exams/show costumes and you wonder why no one appears to have read it!

2 **Don't Make Me Think**. If you make your message or website anything other than completely simple you will be unable to get your message across. There is a reason websites are designed in a similar format. It works! So there is no point in trying to be different or creative if you want people to have easy access to your information. If your viewer has to think about how to navigate your website they will probably lose interest well before they have signed up. Always make navigation quick and simple and REMEMBER it is probably being viewed on a tablet or smart phone so it really is important to get your message across very clearly.

3 Ensure your name and logo are visible, clear and appear in the top third of the page. This rule applies to websites and posters as well as adverts, business cards and any printed materials.

Your brand should always appear above any other brand. IT MUST BE THE MOST IMPORTANT FEATURE.

4 Remember your brand colours and style. They should run through all your communications. Do not send out "mixed messages". Everything should have the look and feel of your brand.

5 Your **USP** (**U**nique **S**elling **P**roposition) should be very clear in all your communications as well as on your website. It really is crucial that prospective students are easily able to see why YOUR school is the best.

6 Your web address, email and/or phone number must appear on every page and be repeated as often as possible. This comes back to number two. **Don't make me think.** Make sure your contact information is readily available no matter who is looking at what!

7 Where possible, avoid a white typeface. Many people find it much more difficult to read this meaningfully, so aim for black, or very dark, text if possible on a white or light coloured background.

8 Use a clear simple typeface. Once again, make it EASY for people to read your message. Aim to

use just one or two different typefaces which then become part of your brand. Avoid the use of "script" – it is much more difficult to read than plain type even though you may feel it looks artistic or friendly. This is all about attracting more people in to your business and then retaining them so make it as easy as possible to read.

9 "Talk" to just one person at a time. Rather than saying, "I hope you are all looking forward to the show," it has a much greater impact if you say, "I hope YOU are looking forward to the show". Or, "your child," rather than, "all the children". Because your message is more personal there is a much greater chance of it being taken personally, so any instructions should be understood... and may even be followed!

10 You generally have only three seconds to grab the attention of your reader. So it really is extremely important to get your message across clearly and simply.

11 In view of this very short time frame, always use a Heading and a PS if you are writing a letter. They could well be the only things that get read! You can use a PS on an email too but ensure it does not get caught up in your signature.

12 For the same reason, a simple but effective subject heading is essential for emails. Keep it short but use words that will capture the attention of the reader and make it stand out from the hundreds of other messages that may be in their inbox.

13 To really be certain your message is being fully understood you need to repeat the same message three times. Tell people you are going to tell them. Tell them, and then tell them you told them! However, it is also important to keep to the same message and not send too many different messages which will only turn in to overload and probably nothing at all will be read or noted!

14 If you have lots of information to impart at the same time it is worth considering bullet points. Short points are much easier to remember than a vast sea of words which many people will probably choose to read "when they have time". For a busy working parent with several children that may be never!

15 You should use a different "tone of voice" in different marketing areas. An email to parents or a post on Linked-In should be more formal than a post on Facebook or Twitter. Imagine one

person in front of you when you are composing your message.

16 Keep all words to a minimum. Especially for posters or other paper marketing. Less is definitely more.

17 If you are printing anything at all, ensure you print on the reverse of the paper too. The greatest expense is the cost of the paper or card so USE BOTH SIDES.

18 You can never proofread too many times! Try and have someone who does not know your business to proofread, as they will need you to have clearly written your message in order for them to understand it. And then proof it again, and again!

19 Do not assume people know what you are talking about. Make everything as clear and simple as possible. You know what a show involves and which theatre you use because you have been producing shows for years. A parent who is new to the school may not know the theatre or even understand just what is involved in your production. Never mind "hair in a bun" (think about it!).

20 Use correct grammar. No slang! If you are not sure, ask someone to check for you. Spellcheck does not always realise the difference between their and there or where and we're.

21 Always include a "Call to Action". Make sure you tell people exactly what you require them to do. "Call today" or "Book now" will make them focus on what is important.

22 Facebook, Twitter, Linked-In, Google places. These are all FREE. Use them! With Google places you should especially be certain that you are listed in all the venues in which you teach or your competitors may be listed instead of you.

23 Networking. This is generally free and YOU are probably the best person to market your own business. Your passion for what you do will always shine through so get those business cards in your pocket, purse or bag and start networking.

24 PR (Public Relations) is free too! Build a relationship with a named person at your local newspaper or magazine. The days of sending a reporter or photographer are long since over, but if you can submit a clear photograph with a write-up the chances are, they will be thrilled to

have that spare newspaper or magazine slot filled with some local, topical news. Aim to send something once a month. It's FREE!

25 Your local radio or TV station may well be interested too. As long as you prepare all the information and email it to them you will be surprised at just how much free marketing is available.

26 If this is all too much to remember just aim to focus on points one and two and my final thought is:

KISS. Keep **I**t **S**hort and **S**imple and there should be a greater understanding from the people who read your messages and communications.

Although you probably think of marketing being all about social media or adverts, one of your most powerful marketing tools will be your show, production or recital. This is an absolutely brilliant way to showcase your school and business to the local community as well as enabling young students in your school to be inspired and motivated by their peers. Many children will take on extra classes once they have seen other students performing something new or different to the dance styles they currently learn.

Make sure local press and radio know when and where your show will be held and send them regular updates – preferably with photographs. Publicise the selling of tickets and make it easy for the whole community to purchase tickets. Use a professional website to sell your tickets. This should still reflect your brand and give an efficient service to all. https://stagestubs.com is worth investigating.

Make It Happen!

1 **KISS** (Keep it short and simple.)
2 **WIFM** (What's in it for me?)
3 Use both sides of the paper when printing.
4 "Talk" to one person at a time
5 Ensure your brand is always obvious.

Chapter 7

Let's Stop CCP

So many dance teachers **Constantly Criticise Parents**! This must stop! Are we not killing the goose that lays the golden egg? Without parents (or guardians) we have NO STUDENTS! It is the parents who pay our salary, enable us to pay our studio rent and generally enable us to run our business. I realise that there will always be one or two parents who are challenging or late payers but, on the whole, parents do support our schools, so let's stop being so negative about them.

By **Constantly Criticising Parents** we build problems that can so easily become self-fulfilling so we need to put an end to **CCP** once and for always!

Although we think we are communicating clearly and professionally with our students, parents or guardians, so often we are not. We know we have told them several times what the show date is, or the exam rehearsal time, but have we really made it clear to them. Because you ALWAYS have your show at the end of March, for example, you might have only said the actual dates once and probably some parents will have missed that message. It is vital that you are consistent in all your messages and that you keep them simple and to the point.

Don't give information overload and remember that bullet-points are often much quicker to read and may make the information easier to retain. If you write great long messages of text, many people will have switched off by line two or three. Even though they know it is important, if there is information overload they will either forget what they have read or will not read it at all.

It is also important to remember that many parents will have other children who may have lots of other interests and so make sure your information is clearly branded so parents know that it is the dance class coaching they need to attend on Tuesday and not the extra football session or the extra French class!

The easier you can make life for the parents the better their response will be and always give your information in a clear and professional manner. If you use some of the marketing and communication pointers in the last chapter you will be certain to have better informed parents and students.

What about the parents who complain? They never do it in their own child's class time... they always try and talk to you just as you are starting your next class! Always smile and thank them for bringing the point to your attention. That generally amazes people! It can also stop them in their tracks if they are being aggressive or rude.

Do not rise to their bait, but stay calm and professional. Explain to them that it is important that they discuss this problem with you and invite them to meet you for a coffee (or even a phone call, but a face to face meeting is always best) within a couple of days, but be specific. Say, "How about meeting me (preferably in the studio or your office if you have one) for a coffee at 10.30 on Tuesday morning?" rather than a vague idea of when. Generally by the time you meet they will have calmed down and probably realised it wasn't such an important issue after all.

Once people know you are willing to listen they will feel less need to try and make contact at inappropriate times. And it should be remembered that your students can only be discussed with their own parents or guardians, so do not get drawn (or allow your staff to be drawn) into conversations about other children.

Another reason for **CCP** is the late-at-night texts, phone calls and emails. Dear teachers, this is completely your own fault! Parents, like their children, need boundaries too! Tell everyone your Business Hours. Feature that information on your website and then only answer the phone or respond to messages during those times. An out of office message or voicemail should be used outside of those hours explaining when they can expect a response.

However, you must also remember that we live in an age of 24/7 communication. Everyone is used to being able to place an order on line with Amazon, or many other companies, at midnight or two in the morning. Possibly this is the best time for a parent to contact you, when all the children are in bed and they finally have time to message you. They SHOULD be able to email, text or message you at any time to suit them, but they will not expect an immediate response. If you have given out your personal email and telephone number then you have no one to blame but yourself!

For the sake of your family, as well as your sanity, you must have a separate business mobile phone. This can be a cheap pay-as-you-go phone that holds all your important contact details but it means you can switch it to voicemail outside of "office hours".

Likewise your business email as well as your business Facebook page can be programmed to send an "out of office" message. You can then respond at a time that suits you, your business and your family. Always having up to date information on your website will help too, as people will get used to checking the website before they ask you.

This all sends out positive and professional messages to everyone who contacts you and makes you appear to be a professional business rather than a "hobby" dance school. You are a professional, having trained for years and are probably still continuing your own professional development, so always ensure everything you do is professional and business-like.

Another CCP issue can arise if you have one or two very strong-minded parents in your school. The longer you have been teaching, the easier it will be to handle them, but remember, do not just criticise them – do something about it. If they are being extremely disruptive then it may be best to just ask them to leave. You may occasionally lose a great pupil but you will NEVER lose a great parent! Better still, try and harness their talents for the good of your school. They could become fervent supporters.

The more professional your business and the more business-like you are, the less of a problem you will have with disruptive parents as they will know where the boundaries lie.

CCP can eat away at us, so eventually it becomes a much greater issue than it really is. Put things in perspective. How many parents in your school are actually causing real problems? Hopefully the answer to that question is "just one or two". If there are many more then you really do need to take a look at some of your policies and procedures and make sure you are adhering to them.

Once you have put these boundaries in place you will discover you have much more time for your family and friends and better quality "you" time too. This is vitally important for your sanity and the wellbeing of your family as well as your friendships. Everybody needs downtime and time to just "be you".

It is also worth remembering the old Chinese proverb:

"One of the first signs of madness is to continue to do the same thing and yet expect a different outcome."

If you want things to improve YOU have to make some changes.

Make It Happen!

1   Remember: You need these parents. They pay the fees!
2   If you don't have work and personal phones, BUY AN EXTRA ONE NOW.
3   Advertise your "office hours" and set voicemails and out of office messages for all other times.
4   Accept the fact that parents want to contact you when it suits them.
5   Your family time and "you" time are important too.

Chapter 8

Policies, Procedures and Contracts

So this is not the "fun" part of running your dance business. However they are all an essential part of ANY business and, generally speaking, once you have set them up you only need to give them a refresh once a year. Put a date in your diary to – choose a quieter time of year, and then DO IT! Every year. You will feel so accomplished once you have completed this.

Policies are many and varied. Some of these you are required to have by law and others are good practice. They will vary from time to time and in different countries.

A **procedure** is a series of steps, taken together, to achieve a desired result. So you need to have procedures in place in order to ensure that your policies actually happen. For example, it is no use to your business if you have a Health and Safety Policy in place but no one understands the procedure to follow if an accident should happen, or if there is a hazard in your studio.

Policies should reflect your brand and ethos as well as actually having your school name and logo on them. Most of your policies should be readily accessible to everyone and consistent in their message. Your website is the ideal place to display them, but ensure they are "read only" versions (or potentially someone else could make changes!).

In Chapter Two, I touched on some policies you should, or must, consider.

If you do not already have these in place you must consider:

- Health and Safety Policy (including risk-assessment).
- Child Protection/Safeguarding Policy.
- Equal Opportunities Policy.
- GDPR/Data Protection Policy.
- Cookie Policy.
- Customer Service Policy.
- Grievance Policy.
- Code of Professional Conduct.

Templates and examples of policies for use in UK may be found here (but please remember to add your own business name and branding!):

http://www.hse.gov.uk/simple-health-safety/write.htm

https://learning.nspcc.org.uk/safeguarding-child-protection/writing-a-safeguarding-policy/

https://www.gov.uk/browse/employing-people

http://www.acas.org.uk

https://cdmt.org.uk/part-time-learning/apply-now

For readers in Scotland:

https://www.bgateway.com/business-guides has loads of useful advice and most countries will offer this sort of support from their government website.

These are just examples and do not reflect the legal requirements of the UK or any other country.

If you are staging shows or taking young people to events then there will be many more considerations which will require policies and procedures. Once again, it may be useful to look at the UK government website: https://www.gov.uk/apply-for-child-performance-licence

If you employ staff then you will need to have a Contract of Employment or a Contract for Self Employed or Freelance staff as well as a Continuing Professional Development Policy. Examples of policies for dance teachers in the UK are readily available from The CDMT (Council for Dance, Drama and Musical Theatre) www.CDMT.org.uk but please remember to personalise them for your own business!

Procedures need to be in place in order to be certain that the correct steps are taken to ensure a desired outcome. For example, if you are planning to employ someone to work at your studio in England, you will need to make sure you have a procedure in place which proves that you have checked the following:

- That they are legally allowed to work in the UK.
- That you have an appropriate contract which you have both signed.
- That suitable insurance is in place.
- That they have a current DBS.
- That you have explained about your H&S Policy and they know how to do a risk assessment if necessary, and understand what to do in an emergency or in case of an accident.

No doubt there will be other items you would add to this induction list and this will vary in different countries and at different times.

Having competitors in your local area can be a really great incentive for you to run your business even better than in the past, but you really do not want them on your doorstep. This is why having a non-compete clause in all teacher contracts is essential. It is often difficult to pursue through the courts if the worst does happen but at least a contract should make someone think about leaving you and setting up their own business nearby. If it does happen, you just need to be very certain everyone in your community know what your USP (Unique Selling Proposition) is, and why your school is the best. The best business will always win in the end.

Having a contract in place for your staff or self-employed freelancers is pretty obvious, but you should also have a contract in place for the following:

- The parents or guardians of your students, which can include such items as a notice period, fee payment, uniform, plus your other expectations. This should be signed at the time the new student enrols and could also include the payment of an enrolment or membership fee. If you do not charge an enrolment fee you are missing a great opportunity to cover some of the expense of legislation, licenses, etc. which are now a large cost to your business.

- Any halls you hire. This will also help to prevent other dance teachers hiring the same hall you use (even if it is on a different night). To the hall administrator, someone teaching Street Dance may be very different to someone teaching Ballet, but we all know that it is very easy for the new teacher to expand their range of classes and suddenly you have a serious competitor in the venue that you have been hiring for many years. A contract could save all this potential hassle and heartache. Have your own contract ready to sign when you start using a new venue in case they do not have one readily available.

- Simple contracts should also be in place for your office manager, chaperones, matrons, photographers and anyone else who comes in to contact with your students whilst they are in your school. Photographs of your work or costumes should be copyright protected and it may also be worth protecting your choreography in a similar way. If you wish to pursue this, the expertise of an IP (Intellectual Property) lawyer will be appropriate.

Always make sure contracts are signed by both parties and a copy is kept securely by you.

The more you think of your school as a business, the more you are likely to consider the time will be well spent setting up some of these procedures. Once they are in place, they should be reviewed annually.

Make It Happen!

1 Check all policies are in place and up-to-date.
2 Check all contracts are in place, up-to-date and signed.
3 Check your procedures are adhered to by all members of the team.
4 Do all policies reflect your brand?
5 No enrolment fee? Introduce one NOW!

Chapter 9

The Numbers Game

Well, of course, it is not a game but having at least a basic understanding of the financial aspects of your business need not be as terrifying as you think it is!

If you have an accountant, they will hopefully save you in tax at least as much as you pay them in fees. If you have an accountant but do not feel they are adequately supporting your business, then either get to know them, or get another accountant who you can work with to grow and develop your school.

Whether you have a book-keeper, accountant or a family member who looks after the financial aspects of your business, it is still vitally important that you have an understanding of where all your income comes from and where all the money actually goes. Hopefully you are doing this either through your school software system or even just using basic Excel spreadsheets, but you absolutely must know the basics.

- **Do you know** your annual turnover?

- **Do you know** the annual gross and net profit figures?

- **ARE YOU ACTUALLY MAKING A PROFIT?**

- **Do you know** how many new students you would need to pay for a five percent increase in your studio rental costs?

- **Do you know** the real costs of employing a new assistant teacher (include all the extras like any CPD (Continuing Professional Development) training you pay for, as well as workplace pensions, holiday pay, travel costs, etc.)?

- **Remember: You are running a BUSINESS.**

Are all your classes profitable? If you only have a handful of students in some classes, you are unlikely to be even covering your costs, let alone running at a profit. The temptation is to just carry on, always hoping that some new students will turn up. But this is unlikely to happen unless you CHANGE something. So you must either change the class content, encourage more students or close the class.

The latter may be a difficult decision but you should be making decisions which are right for your business and its future and not just what is right for one or two students at that particular time. You are also sending out the wrong message to everyone if there are just a couple of students in a class as it will be obvious to everyone that this is not a profitable business. From the teachers point of view, it is pretty demoralising to only teach a few students and it is not great for the pupils themselves to be in such a tiny class.

Any classes that are not profitable should be analysed to see what you can do to increase numbers. Remember the old Chinese proverb:

"One of the first signs of madness is to continue to do the same thing and yet expect a different outcome."

If you want more profitable classes you have to change something.

Just because you have never had adult classes in your school, should not mean that you never consider them in the future. If that is what people in your area are looking for, then start some adult classes, even if you have to find a new teacher. Alternatively you or a colleague should be able to find a good CPD (Continuing Professional Development) course or seminar where you could learn a new style or technique.

There will always be something new to teach if you want to expand your business but you might just have to think a little differently. Try and find a genre that others are not teaching. Your competitors may well copy your initiative, but at least you will be the first in your area to try something new.

If your competitor does get there first, do not be afraid to teach a similar style as it could well become a new trend. Just be sure to call it something different and teach in a slightly different way so you still keep a differentiation between you and the other school.

Does your school offer private lessons? If so, have you taken in to account all the costs involved including studio hire, travel costs, teacher's fee, preparation time for choreography etc., before deciding on the hourly rate? The same applies to exam coaching or show rehearsals. This is all part of your business – you are not running a charity!

It is always a good idea to make small increases in your fees on an annual basis. Parents and students will then know in advance and can budget accordingly. If there is no increase for several years it could be difficult to suddenly substantially increase the fees to cover a rent rise or some other unforeseen costs.

Your enrolment or membership fee should also be increased from time to time. If you do not currently charge either then you are missing a great opportunity. Most groups, societies, clubs and organisations now charge either an annual "membership" fee or a one-off enrolment fee. Make this a payment to secure the student's place but do not then give them a "free" T-shirt which negates the cost. Remember you are running a business!

If you are worried about how to implement it, consider just charging new students into your school – they will not know any different. You can explain it is to cover insurance, licences, or anything you wish, but most parents will expect some sort of joining fee as that is what many other associations or companies charge.

Even if you have full capacity in your school, it is still important that you understand the costs. It is very easy to be extremely busy and yet not profitable. Always remember: **Turnover is vanity. Profit is sanity.**

If you have a full class but the costs of the studio and teacher are more than the income for that actual session, this is not profitable and is therefore not good business practice. This can easily happen if you hire a specialist or celebrity teacher, so keep an eye on those costs!

Assuming you are making a profit, you will need to pay tax regardless of whether you are self-employed, a sole-trader, a limited company or partnership. Help and support is available free for businesses in the UK from https://www.gov.uk/log-in-register-hmrc-online-services

How sustainable is your business?

- If you were suddenly unable to use your venue could you afford to rent somewhere else?

- If you are renting premises do you have a valid and signed contract or lease? If not, you are living very dangerously! The venue owner could easily increase your rent substantially and with very little notice if you do not have a signed contract.

- If your main teacher suddenly became ill, could you afford to pay a "supply" teacher?

And the opposite could happen too: Could you cope if a primary school opened near your studio and scores of children wanted to sign up? Do you have the space and teaching staff to support extra growth?

The sustainability of your business is something you should consider and perhaps even consider a Business Continuity Plan, just in case the worst should ever happen. If your venue was destroyed by fire or unusable due to flooding, do you have alternative studio space available to you?

Are you insured for loss of earnings if you were unable to teach? If you sustained an injury or became seriously ill and were unable to teach you might still be liable for your rent and other business expenses. Could your business sustain this loss and continue?

There are many "worst case scenarios" that should be considered by all responsible business owners.

From time to time, most schools will have someone who defaults on the payment of their fees. The more business-like your school, the less likely this is to happen. If this situation does arise then you must address it *immediately*.

You must implement whatever your terms and conditions or parent contract states. If you send a letter or email as a reminder, print the second one in RED ink and call it a "letter before action". If that still does not work then use the small claims court. Help and templates (often free) are available online for both of these. It may seem harsh, but it is crucial that you act on your policy or terms, not least so that others know you will not be "taken for a ride" by their non-payment. After all, if you go to a supermarket and pick up some bread and milk and tell the cashier, "I'll drop the money in next week," it's called stealing and the perpetrator will end up with a criminal record. Most parents would never steal from a store, so why should they steal from your business?

You may consider joining FSB (The Federation of Small Businesses) https://www.fsb.org.uk as part of their membership you will be able to send up to 20 FREE solicitor's letters each year. Just one of those could recover more than your annual membership fee! Check their website for more details. Your membership will also allow you to meet other local businesses and provide some great networking opportunities.

There are "hidden" costs in many businesses. What do you think yours might be? If you work from home it is especially easy to overlook many minor office costs, although there can also be potential capital gains tax issues if you claim for too much. The advice of your accountant will definitely be worth seeking here.

Remember to claim for all your expenses relating to your CPD (continuing professional development) and exam days can have many hidden costs. Show time can be a minefield and it is worth considering a separate bank account for show costumes, lighting, theatre hire etc. so you can easily see exactly where the costs are accruing.

As well as teaching, another way to generate income is, of course, by selling your uniform dancewear and accessories. This can be done either through your own school website or by making arrangements with a local dance shop to pay you a commission on orders from your school. Not only does it ensure your students wear the correct uniform for their class but having all students dressed correctly will keep your brand strong. It will also give a sense of belonging for the students which will help to retain them within your school.

Take some time to understand the figures relating to your business. Familiarise yourself with all the hidden costs as well as the obvious ones. Seek help from your accountant if necessary and you will have a greater understanding of your business as well as its finances. The more financially secure your business becomes the more sustainable its future. You are more likely to be able to secure a buyer for it, if that is part of your plan, and you will potentially have more freedom to give back more to your local community or dancers who are in need of financial support.

Make It Happen!

1   What is your annual turn-over?
2   Check all your classes are profitable.
3   Plan to increase fees annually.
4   Introduce a membership or enrolment fee.
5   Stop being frightened of the figures!

Chapter 10

Automation

Life can be much simpler if you take some time to add some automation into your schedule.

Posting on your social media accounts is valuable for customer engagement as well as invaluable for reminding everyone about when you require certain things to happen. Instead of trying to always remember to do this at the appropriate time why not **schedule** your posts? It will be worth planning them in advance and schedule them to post at the time you know most people will read them.

Before scheduling anything, it is worth taking some time to experiment with the best time to post or to send an email. If you always post at 10.00 pm then try some posts in the morning or afternoon or even on different days. The time and day can make a dramatic difference as to who actually reads your posts or opens the emails you send.

You can plan a schedule days, weeks or months ahead. Although it might take some time initially it is a wonderful feeling when you realise you are ahead of the game!

Social media accounts can be linked for ease if you wish. https://buffer.com is a free app which will help you to do this and there are other apps available too. https://mailchimp.com will help you to design, plan and schedule emails. It is GDPR (General Data Protection Regulation) compliant and FREE to use. You can also track the emails and when and how often they were opened.

Presumably you are using some kind of class management software to run your business. The systems are many and varied and the price varies considerably too. You should research the market and talk to a number of the companies. Examples are:

- https://classmanager.com
- https://www.thinksmartsoftware.com/en-gb/products/dancebiz/overview.html
- https://www.membermeister.com

plus there are many other systems available.

If you already have a software system in place then check to make sure you are making the most of its capabilities.

Possibly when you first installed it you needed to just use the basics but if you are paying for a comprehensive system then make sure you are using everything you can. If you are confused about any aspect most companies will be only too happy to respond to you queries and talk you through any problems you may be having.

You can sell dancewear from your website direct to your parents at no cost to you. If you really want to save time but still make a profit on your sales then https://www.mydancestore.co.uk is certainly worth investigating. It links to your website, is fully branded with your own logo and only the products you want your students and parents to see will be visible. You earn commission on all sales and have all your students in the correct uniform. Bonus!

Do you sell tickets for you school show or recital? It can be a real headache, or it can be really simple if you use https://stagestubs.com. This ticketing system can also be used for summer school classes, one-off special events and all manner of performances. There are no set-up costs and the money goes straight into your bank account every time a ticket is sold. What not to like!

Remember to also automate your "out of office" responses for emails and Facebook as well as your voicemail message. Tell people when they can expect a response from you. As well as giving a professional and business-like look to your brand it keeps people informed. This is vital if you want them to be engaged with your company.

Fully embracing automation will give your business a more professional look and feel. It will possibly save you a lot of hassle and a great deal of uncertainty. It will ultimately give you much more time which means you save on your costs too.

More professionalism for your business. More time for you.

Make It Happen!

1   Schedule your social media posts.
2   Schedule emails in advance.
3   Investigate or update class software systems.
4   Sell dancewear via your website.
5   Sell your tickets on-line.

Chapter 11

When You Reach For The Stars...

Having read this far, I sincerely hope that you are feeling more positive about your business. I hope you realise the amazing contribution you are making to society, and I also hope you are now in a position to grow and develop your business and your school. The dance industry is an incredible industry and we are privileged to be a part of it.

Once you have a sound business base for your enterprise, the opportunities are endless. Once you have established the foundations, you can achieve so many other dreams and ambitions and continue to have a positive impact on the lives of so many people.

Keep alive the passion that made you want to teach dance in the first place. Dance teachers have a massive impact on the lives of their students, and often the parents as well. It is an amazing gift to be able to pass on your love for this wonderful art form.

Always remember that not everyone we teach will become another prima ballerina or Fred Astaire. But maybe they will take their own children to watch dance or to join a dance class, thus ensuring there will be jobs for dancers and dance teachers for many more generations to come. What a legacy!

As a dance teacher you have created many poised, disciplined, well-mannered young people who will go through life understanding how to work as a team – because of you.

They will realise that, through hard work and diligent practice anything is possible – because of you.

They will know that dreams really can come true – because of you.

Because this is what dance teachers do. Day in, day out. Let us share our knowledge, our professionalism and our passion with each other, so that, eventually, dance teachers everywhere will be respected as the hugely important professionals within society that they actually are.

And finally: please remember to keep growing your dreams, your goals and your vision as well as keeping alive the passion that you have for this wonderful industry, and you will undoubtedly Grow Your Dance Business.

In the iconic lyrics of Anthony Drewe from his stage version of *Mary Poppins*:

> "If you reach for stars
> All you get are the stars
> But we've found a whole new spin
> If you reach for the Heavens
> You get the stars thrown in."

About The Author

At the age of eight my mother took me to see the ballet *Sleeping Beauty* at the Royal Court Theatre in Liverpool, it changed my life. "I wanted to be the lilac fairy", I was totally spellbound! I immediately asked my Mother if I could have ballet lessons and soon decided I wanted to be a ballet teacher.

I was born and brought up in Crosby, Liverpool, where my father was a window cleaner and my mother a school teacher. I left school at 16 to go to dance college and very soon was giving dance classes in the local church hall in order to make the money to pay for my own dance training. By the time I was 21, I was renting a dance studio of my own where I taught 150 pupils ballet, tap and modern dance, I had absolutely no money, I scraped together the rent and that was it.

When the keep fit boom arrived a few years later, I also started offering keep fit classes for adults. By 1979 I had moved to bigger studios and had two teachers working for me. I also started making bright coloured leotards for my pupils to wear in the end-of-term shows I put on at the local theatre.

Most people at that time still wore black or blue nylon leotards and they didn't fit like leotards do now, they were baggy, lumpy garments and I hated seeing my students looking like that, but I realised there was this amazing fabric you could get in bright colours called Lycra. My leotards were soon in demand and a lot of my friends were dance teachers, so they would see them in my shows and ask me to make them some. Initially, I made the leotards on a friend's sewing machine as a favour to other teachers, but as the demand grew I borrowed £50 from my mother and bought an old industrial sewing machine, which I installed in a friend's attic.

The school was expanding, so I made them at all sorts of bizarre times, sometimes during the day and sometimes late in the evening after class. Harlequin Dancewear (now International Dance Supplies or IDS) was born!

In 1980 I married a Devon man, but continued to run my dance school and make leotards in Crosby during the week and commuted to Devon at the weekend. By 1985 I decided it was time to move to Devon permanently so I handed over the dance school to a friend and took my sewing machine with me!

By now the dancewear business was a separate entity, I was selling to dance teachers and retailers all over the country. In Devon I hired a small unit on an industrial site for £35 a week, to begin with I was on my own – I would sew the leotards myself and then phone round to get orders, sometimes I would close the place to go and deliver them. In the first year I had sales of £15,000. I took on a couple of machinists and a youth training scheme trainee and when my Husband Tony retired, he joined the business too.

Over the years we grew IDS to be one of the biggest local employers distributing our dancewear and costumes around the world. It is wonderful for me to see it continuing to grow and thrive and it has just celebrated its 40th birthday!

During all these years I stayed in touch with dance teachers as I was the RAD (Royal Academy of Dance) local organiser for the North-West and then the South-West where I was also Chair of the Region at one time. I was instrumental in founding both the North-West and South-West IDTA (International Dance Teachers Association) Areas and was the first Chairman of the North-West Area. I became a trustee of the RAD and was a member of their finance committee for many years and I am currently a trustee of CDMT (Council for Dance, Drama & Musical Theatre). I am a Life Member of ISTD

(Imperial Society of Teachers of Dance) and an Honorary Member of bboDance (formerly the British Ballet Organisation).

Many of the achievements at IDS were driven by the hopes and dreams I had as a dance teacher and one of my passions is to share the business knowledge I have learnt over so many years with dance teachers and other business owners.

In 2010 I was delighted to be honoured with an MBE for Services to Business in the Queen's Birthday Honours and I have also been awarded a First Women Award, Everywoman Award and a Stevie Entrepreneur Award. I am proud to be a Patron of Devon Rape Crisis & Sexual Abuse Services as well as Tap Attack.

Lightning Source UK Ltd.
Milton Keynes UK
UKHW040646291118
333105UK00001B/46/P